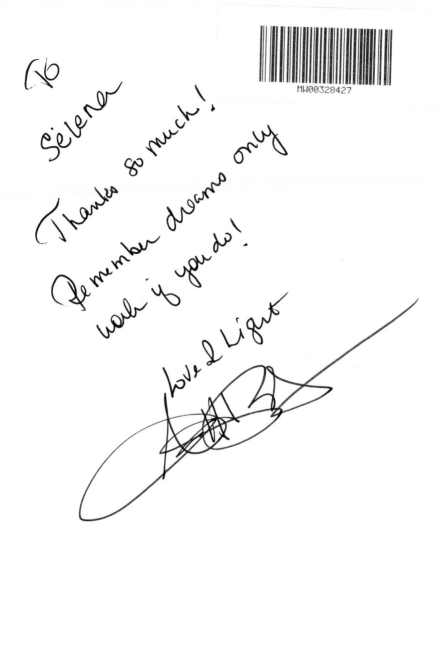

To
Selena
Thanks so much!
Remember dreams only
work if you do!

Love & Light

THINK LIKE A
BOSS

31 Tips to Grow Your Brand
from the Inside Out

ALEXANDRA BERNARD-SIMMONS

DEDICATION

THIS BOOK IS DEDICATED TO MY YOUNGER SELF. THANK you for not allowing the world to change your dream. Thank you for always staying positive in the face of adversity, and thank you for never giving up.

TABLE OF CONTENTS

INTRODUCTION

"Your idea is a seed—you can choose to water it or let it die." — *Alexandra*

AS KIDS WE WERE FULL OF CRAZY IDEAS. WHAT'S EVEN crazier is the fact that we acted on those ideas. We leaped from coffee table to couch, slid down the stairs on our bottoms, and jumped off garage roofs. As adults we have some great ideas, too, but we refuse out of fear to take the risk we did when we were kids. When did we lose our courage?

This book is going to help merge childlike dares of dreaming big and adult mannerisms to form what are known as calculated risks. Let's face it—building a business and following your dreams can be scary. But always remember that fear is a liar. It hinders us from becoming our best selves. Becoming your own boss and breaking the chains of the normalcy of working for someone else seems like a stretch, but it can be done. Other people are doing this, so why not you?

These tips will help you in every level of your business and ignite your light so you can follow your passion with more calculated moves. As an efficacious entrepreneur I personally have used these tips to build not one but three separate successful brands and landed me opportunities to appear on numerous big-name TV networks! With this book, being fearful of taking risks is now a thing of the past. You're now on the right path for your entrepreneurial journey, and this book will help make your risk a little less daunting.

"Mind is everything. Muscle: pieces of rubber. All that I am, I am because of my mind." – Paavo Nurmi, Olympic Legend

TIP #31

MENTALLY PREPARE YOURSELF.

THE ENTREPRENEURIAL JOURNEY CAN BE EXCITING AND rewarding, but it can also cause high levels of stress. How do you combat this? Prepare yourself mentally and build a regimen of good habits. Studies show that one habit shared between highly successful people is a very consistent and effective morning ritual to start their day with a highly focused mind. This ritual can include reading, yoga, meditation, prayer, affirmations, goal setting … the list goes on.

What are you feeding yourself mentally on a daily basis? Do you nourish your soul the same way you nourish your body? If the answer is no, then this is the first thing that should go in effect as of yesterday. Your life is a manifestation of your thoughts: If you are filling your head with doubt and negative self-talk, then you and you alone are holding yourself back from greatness.

An easy way to get into this habit is to create daily affirmations or mantras that embody your future goals and the characteristics that will help you achieve your dream. Once you come up with the perfect combination, repeat this to yourself daily. Say your affirmations in the morning and at night, when you are at your highest point or when you are feeling stressed. Most importantly, say it with conviction. For example, a strong mantra can't start with "I will" or "I am going to" because this implies that you don't have it. So instead of saying "I will make six figures utilizing my passions," say "I make six figures utilizing my passions." This way you are already owning the goal, "like attracts like" and the Law of Attraction will bring this into your universe.

This practice worked for me time and time again since I was a teenager. If you open my yearbook from my senior year, under my picture it boldly states I planned to open my own dance school. I truly believed I would, and as I went through young adulthood, college, marriage, children, single motherhood, and more, I still built the experience and accumulated the knowledge to open my own dance school, Evolution of Hip-Hop, LLC, nine years after my senior year of high school. The intent was always clear. In 2016 we have two locations and have a third in the works.

Speaking my future as a business owner into existence as a senior in high school and by having it printed in my yearbook under my portrait was just the start for me. By affirming my goals, including the fact that I would make six figures while pursuing my passion, I watch my goals manifest themselves right before my eyes. Because I believed I could, I did.

All that you are, you are because of your mind. Get your mind right.

"Average people earn money doing things they don't love. Rich people follow their passion." — Steve Siebold

TIP #30

MAKE YOUR PASSION MARKETABLE.

CHASING MONEY HAS BECOME MORE POPULAR NOWA-days than chasing dreams. That's fine if you enjoy the endless race. If you are looking for a fulfilling life, however, remember that your passions lead you to your purpose, and once you are walking in purpose the money will come. So how do you make sure your passions will bring in dollars? Use these questions to get your creative juices flowing to ensure you can make your passion marketable.

What do I like to do with my time?

What do others say I'm good at?

Do I have hobbies or interests that are marketable?

Is my idea practical, and will it fill a need?

What is my advantage over similar businesses?

What services or products will I sell based on my passion?

Will I still love this ten years from now?

If you are not a business owner already, the answers to these questions will help you get started on making your idea a reality. Keep in mind that your purpose should always serve the greater good. If your idea helps solve a problem or a fulfill need, then you're on the right track.

As an example, take the CEO of Annie's Delights, a baking company based in the New York Tri-State area. Annie started as an artist. Even though she enjoyed drawing and creating paintings, this work didn't necessarily fill a need for the masses. When she transformed her craft into creating cake masterpieces, she was able to touch thousands of people with custom artwork for their special occasions. "When my customers start to break down in tears over their wedding or baby shower cake, I just thank God that I can share my talent with the world in this way," says Annie.

Narrow down the work you love to do—work that makes your soul smile—and turn it into a business. Remember that you're chasing the dream, not the money.

"If you are not willing to learn, no one can help you. If you are determined to learn, no one can stop you." – Zig Ziglar

TIP #29

EDUCATE YOURSELF, BECOME THE EXPERT.

"KNOWLEDGE IS POWER" HAS GOT TO BE ONE OF THE most well-known sayings of all time. This is one of the reasons you picked up this book! But what are you doing to learn about the industry of your business? Would you consider yourself an expert in the field? Make sure you are staying on top of the trends of your business. For example, owners of hair salons are always learning new ways to keep their clients current with today's hairstyles.

How much do you know when it comes to the different aspects of your business? For the first year or so, there's a strong possibility you will be carrying your company on your back 100%. This means you must be your own publicist, accountant, researcher, etc. We are in the time of robust YouTube tutorials and websites like eHow (ehow.com) and Curious (curious.com), which can walk you through any process you need to learn and teach you any skill you need to acquire—if you dedicate the time.

Beyond the Internet, local community colleges often offer classes in many different areas for low prices. Some are available at night or even on weekends to accommodate a working person's busy schedule. Another great way to learn is by going to seminars and workshops focused on your niche. For example, my second company, Think Like a Boss NJ, which was also the inspiration and driving factor of this book, is constantly putting together workshops for women in the New York Tri-State area to teach them different skills in business and in life! For women who are too busy to get out or don't live near one of our events, we host phone webinars to share our message with everyone who wants to hear it. If you would like to join us at our next event or webinar, check our website at www.ActLadyThinkBoss.com for our current schedule.

In this day and age there is no reason why you can't pick up a new skill to help your business. Educate yourself and become unstoppable.

"The best way to avoid distractions is to turn them off." – Peter Bregman

TIP #28

USE YOUR 24 HOURS WISELY.

4.7 HOURS. THAT IS THE AVERAGE TIME A PERSON SPENDS on their phone on any given day. Within that time frame, according to research done by Informate Mobile Intelligence, the average person checks their social media a whopping 17 times a day...or more!

Social media has become part of one's everyday routine, like checking email or checking our mailboxes when we get home, but we tend to get carried away. What would you do if you had an extra 4.7 hours to work on your business?

I know so many successful people who choose not to watch TV, but the one example I'm going to use is billionaire Bill Gates. During an interview with co-founder of Sun Microsystems, Bill stated, "I don't watch TV; there is no money in TV, except of course, if you own the network."

Time management and prioritizing your focus is integral to growing and building your business. Where you spend your time is where your future will be. So instead of binge watching **Empire**, come up with your master plan to build your own empire.

"Oh, I'm sorry. I forgot I only exist when you need something." – *Unknown*

TIP #27

USE THEM, JUST LIKE THEY USE YOU.

WE SPEND ANYWHERE FROM 8 TO 12 HOURS A DAY HELP-ing someone else achieve their dream. They are taking all of our time, forcing us to wear multiple hats to get their job done, making sure we can be efficient under pressure to meet deadlines, and in return we get our paycheck, a few days off, and no job security. Some of you do so much work at work you can run your own business with the experience you've accumulated over the years. Think about it: You have accrued skills like multitasking, customer service, data processing, accounting, problem solving, learning new systems, managing employees, and so on.

Take advantage of all the training, resources, and, experience you currently receive at your present job. Use the printer on your lunch break to print your marketing material and the Internet for research for all I care! All jokes aside, use this time for you, too! Join available clubs like Toastmasters to practice speaking in front of groups, sign up for leadership classes, or take extra training course on work-related software or any new technologies. Get this free knowledge to better yourself as a professional and as a future CEO.

Most importantly, use your job to fund your dream. Entrepreneurs aren't built overnight, and neither are the funds. Start your business while you're still employed and funnel money that you earn into your business. The point is this: While you're at work, make your work place work for you. This is a key factor in the calculated risk of starting a business.

"Planning is bringing the future into the present so that you can do something about it now." – Alan Lakein

TIP #26

DO YOU HAVE A BUSINESS PLAN?

START PUTTING YOUR IDEAS ON PAPER! A BUSINESS PLAN is a formal document explaining in detail your plans to develop a financially successful business. You may need this down the line for funding, but more importantly it helps keep track of the details and forces you to think through EVERY aspect of your business. Below are the sections of a standard business plan. Go to https://www.score.org for a thorough example of what your business plan should like. This website is a great resource for both new and established business owners. Get out there and start planning!

KEY COMPONENTS OF A BUSINESS PLAN:

Executive Summary

Company Description

Market Analysis

Organization and Management

Service or Product Line

Marketing and Sales

Funding Request

Financial Projections

Appendix

"Doing business without advertising is like winking at a girl in the dark. You know what you're doing, but no one else does." – Steuart Henderson Britt

TIP #25

MARKET, THEN MARKET SOME MORE.

YOUR MARKETING BUDGET SHOULD BE ANYWHERE between 10% and 12% of your gross revenue, or as much as 20% for a competitive market or new business! That's a significant part of business spend, yet business owners often fail to plan for these targets. Now that you're reading this tip you know better. When you know better, do better! Let's run through some common marketing channels for your business to avoid this detrimental mistake.

Online Marketing. We all understand that we should have an online presence with a professionally produced website, but online marketing doesn't stop there. Your company should be visible via many local listings and directories, such as Yelp, Bing, Yahoo, YP.com, USDirectory. com, TripAdvisor, and many more. Some of these listings also give you the opportunity to advertise with them. For example, Yelp has a month-to-month program that highlights your business when customers search for your product or services on their website. The most scalable and successful online marketing tools I've ever used as an entrepreneur is search engine optimization with effective keywords. Everyone knows how to do a quick Internet search when they are in need of specific products or services. Heck, one of the most common search engines is now a verb–just "Google" it! With the right keywords linked to your website and effective search engine optimization, you can make sure your company comes up in your potential customers' search results, with links that lead them straight to your website.

Another option to consider when it comes to your online presence is social retail services like Groupon and Living Social. This is a great option because you are not paying any lump sums up front. They do, however, take a significant amount from your bottom line. They first ask you to discount your product or service 50% to draw in the customers, and then take about 20% off of that. Their reach is unparalleled, and customers love to shop through these partners due to discounts and clout. This can be a fantastic way to get exposure for your company, but–and this is a big "but"–do not stay with these partners for too long. In the long run these deep discounts devalue your company and its services because customers will get used to paying half price for what your business has to offer. If you're looking for a short-term boost or need to break into a new market, then consider this route–it can work very well! Learn how to capitalize off that popularity so that you can retain customers and offer a referral system from the customers you gained during this "sale."

Below is a list of some websites you may want information on your business to be available. Online presence is very important!

Answers	Seek it Local	Google
AOL	Tom	MojoPages
Apple	Trip Advisor	Patch
Bing	Twitter	ReachLocal
B2B YellowPages	USDirectory.com	Yahoo
EZLocal.com	Walk Score	Yelp
ForLocations	YellowBook	Living Social
GoLocal247.com	YellowBot	Just Click Local
Groupon	YellowPageCity	Merchant Circle
HotFrog	Mapquest	

Social Media Marketing. Online marketing is cool, but social media marketing is a MUST! Social media is also considered online marketing, but effective use of this marketing channel requires specific know-how and a unique strategy that sets it apart from traditional online marketing.

When it comes to social media, pick your top three favorite platforms and focus on them. If you try to join all of the social media platforms, you will be overwhelmed and get nowhere fast. Once you pick your top three, use apps like Hootsuite to manage several social media pages and posts efficiently. When it comes to posting, create engaging, sharable content to help social media users—they're all customers or potential customers—feel connected to you. Make sure you're always adding value to people's lives with posts that are either motivational or informative. Use hashtags that are relevant and can drive people to your content—an effective hashtag alone can draw 20 or more people to your post. Last but not least, use the paid advertising feature for your business pages. This is available on Facebook, Twitter, and even Instagram. You can target your demographic specifically, right down to their shopping habits and topics they are interested in. This is highly effective and is now the number one way to market a business.

Old Fashion Marketing. During this age of technology we can't forget the oldies but goodies! Get some feet on the street—pass out flyers and have engaging conversations with people. Personally, I get flagged down at the gas station, supermarket, or mall by a potential customer to ask questions about my company because of the ad they just read on the driver's side car door. There are so many activities that still work! Put signs in vacant office buildings, hire truck side advertising, place bus bench ads, set up trade show booths, send direct mail postcards, use wraparound ads on cars, create supermarket checkout placards, post roadside signs, and more. These ideas are simple and cost-effective, and they can still bring customers through the door.

Email Marketing. From your online marketing and social media ads and your flyers around town, there should ALWAYS be a strong call to action: read my blog, sign up, register, etc. This will enable to you build your email list with people you know are or may be interested in your product or services. As you build your email list, these people should get monthly updates, coupons, deals, and more, all of which will drive sales. Email marketing has proven to be very successful and is a great way to stay in touch with past and future customers.

"Laws are spider webs through which big flies pass and the little ones get caught." — Honore de Balzac

TIP #24

TAKE CARE OF LEGALITIES.

LEGAL TROUBLE ISN'T FUN FOR ANYBODY, AND THE SAME goes for your business. You become your business, which means that, depending on how you choose to incorporate, any legal issues with your business will run into your personal affairs. CEO Dominique McCullough told me about what she thought was one of her biggest failures with her natural bath and body product company, Madinina Kiss: Dominique did not trademark her brand (e.g., name, logo, etc.), and she almost lost the rights to the brand that she'd been building for years! Trademarking, incorporating, contracts, permits, and other legal documents should be looked over and filed by a professional.

To give you some basic knowledge, here's a quick breakdown of different incorporations so you can figure out what will work best for you.

OWNERSHIP AND LEGAL STRUCTURES

Sole Proprietorship: A single person owns the business; very most common structure. Profits are taxed as income to the owner personally.

Advantages

- ☐ This is the easiest and least expensive form of ownership to organize.

- ☐ As the owner, you have complete control and may make decisions as you see fit.

- ☐ You receive all income generated by the business to keep or reinvest.

- ☐ The business is easy to dissolve, if desired.

Disadvantages

- ☐ You are often limited to using funds from personal savings or consumer loans.

- ☐ You may have a hard time attracting high-caliber employees or those who are motivated by the opportunity to own a part of the business.

- ☐ Employee benefits, such as the owner's medical insurance premiums, are not directly deductible.

☐ Business income is only partially deductible as an adjustment to personal income.

General Partnership: Similar to sole proprietorship but with two or more people.

OR

Limited Partnership: One partner has more control; others have as much as they put in.

Advantages

- These are relatively easy to establish; however, time should be invested in developing the partnership agreement.

- With more than one owner, the ability to raise funds may be increased.

- The business usually will benefit from partners who have complementary skills.

Disadvantages

☐ All owners are jointly and individually liable for the actions of the other partners.

☐ Profits must be shared with others.

☐ Since decisions are shared, disagreements can occur.

☐ The partnership may have a limited life; it may end upon the withdrawal or death of a partner.

C Corporation: This is a legal entity made up of individuals and is recognized as being a separate entity having its own rights and liabilities.

OR

S Corporation: Special requirements allow the S corporation to be taxed less like a partnership or sole proprietorship.

Advantages

- ☐ Shareholders have limited liability for the corporation's debts or for judgments against the corporations.

- ☐ Shareholders are generally held accountable only for their investment in stock of the company.

- ☐ Additional funds can be raised through the sale of stock.

- ☐ If the requirements for S corporation status are met, then the company to be taxed similar to a partnership.

- ☐ The corporation may deduct the cost of benefits it provides to officers and employees.

Disadvantages

- ☐ The process of incorporation requires more time and money than other forms of organization.

- ☐ Corporations are monitored by federal, state, and some local agencies, and as a result may have to manage more paperwork to comply with regulations.

- ☐ Incorporating may result in higher overall taxes. Dividends paid to shareholders are not deductible from business income, thus it can be taxed twice.

Limited Liability Company (LLC): This structure combines corporate and partnership characteristics while maintaining its status as a legal entity distinct from its owners.

Advantages

- ☐ LLCs require less paperwork compared with C-Corps or S-Corps, and they are very flexible.

- ☐ LLCs provide their members protection from liability, similar to corporations.

Disadvantages

- ☐ Unless you choose to be taxed like a corporation, LLCs are usually subject to self-employment taxes.

- ☐ In many jurisdictions, if a member departs the LLC, the LLC ceases to exist.

If you need some help with some legal services, start with The Company Corporation. They can handle all your start-up services for a great price. Make sure you're running a fully legit and legal business to save you from many headaches, heart aches, and even lawsuits in the future.

"The richest people in the world look for and build networks; everyone else looks for work." — Robert Kiyosaki

TIP #23

YOUR NETWORK IS YOUR NET WORTH.

WE HAVE ALL HEARD THIS SAYING BEFORE, BUT ARE WE taking heed? Going to different events and meeting other professionals strengthens potential business partnerships. Face it: Everyone knows something you don't, and that something can help bring your business to the next level. Going to mixers and networking events should be part of your business strategy. Opportunities come out of great conversations with other dream chasers. Who you know is just as important as what you know.

"There is no professional or personal anymore, there's simply your brand. Everything you do affects your brand and it's up to you to determine whether your brand is affected positively or negatively." – Peter Thanciman

TIP #22

YOU ARE A BRAND 24/7, SO ACT LIKE ONE.

LET'S GET BACK TO BASICS WHEN WE'RE TALKING ABOUT representing your brand. The first thing you must do is master your "elevator pitch." This is a 30-second description of exactly what you do for your customers. Explain to the listener the benefits of choosing your company and what sets you apart from your competition. A solid pitch should have them hooked. Second, you should always have your business cards with you because you never know who is in need of your services. One of the first questions people ask strangers is what they do for work—use that to your advantage and be prepared with these two things.

This tip is important especially for your reputation. Nowadays your actions can come up any and everywhere on social media. This will affect the perception of your company and can influence your customers' decisions. Believe it or not, people like to buy from good people and honest companies. Once they see and hear stories of do-gooders, happy employees, and CEOs with social awareness, it automatically gives your company a positive personality. Customers feel good when they can purchase from a company they can trust. So clean up your act online and offline to be the person you want to represent your brand.

Finally, represent your brand to the eye as well. We all remember Apple CEO Steve Jobs and his signature black turtleneck for every release of a new Apple product, right? It was a simple and sleek look, just like the Apple products. You can do something similar. The logos of two of my three companies, The Evolution of Hip-Hop LLC and I Am Travel Wear, are both yellow. Any time I'm representing my company at an event or on national TV, I always have a touch of yellow in my outfit to tie me right back to my brand.

"Our success has really been based on partnerships from the very beginning." – Bill Gates

TIP #21
PARTNER UP.

ONCE WE BECOME CEOS, WE TURN INTO OVERPROTECTIVE Mama Bears when it comes to sharing our businesses. After all, we gave birth to the idea, and the business is like our baby. As a result we believe we know best at all times. Blindly following this approach, however, can stunt your company's growth. Whether it's a partnership for services or you are bringing in a partner to help you run the business, bringing in partner—an individual or another company—with different skills, resources, or funds can catapult you to the next level.

When it comes to partnerships, make sure you partner with a person or business that matches your spirit. It's best if you and this partners morals, attitude, and views are all aligned. The reputation of your business and your well-being will depend upon the partner you choose to help you raise your baby so choose wisely.

"The power of a book lies in its power to turn a solitary act into a shared vision." – Laura Bush

TIP #20

WRITE A BOOK.

NOTHING SCREAMS EXPERT LIKE BEING A PUBLISHED author! You're automatically more marketable and believable. Writing a book is no easy feat, but once you're done you've expanded your brand to a whole new market of people. Having a tangible book is great when doing speaking events, conferences, or trade shows, and many publishers can make an e-book version available on many platforms, making it easy for readers to find your material. So gather your thoughts, facts, and life stories and get started!

"Publicity is absolutely critical. A good
PR story is infinitely more effective than
a front-page ad." — Richard Branson

TIP #19

GET A PUBLICIST.

GET A PUBLICIST—PERIOD. GETTING YOUR BRAND OUT there so people know about you is all about reach, and that's precisely what a publicist can deliver. A publicist has the ability to help you manage your relationship with the media. He or she can help set up interviews with newspapers, magazines, and other publications, and can also assist with press releases, public appearances, and—most importantly—guide you away from bad publicity. Invest in a publicist to build traction, deepen your reach, and strengthen the image for your brand.

"We make a living by what we get, but we make a life by what we give." – Winston Churchill

TIP #18

CONNECT WITH YOUR COMMUNITY.

YOUR COMMUNITY IS YOUR CUSTOMER. THEY ARE TAKING a chance on you with your products and services, so take a chance for them as well. Become a sponsor for events around your area. Don't stop there! Give back to schools and churches, or start your own program. Your community will vouch for you and can be the best source of word of mouth publicity.

Even though The Evolution of Hip Hop LLC is very involved with local youth and communities, I still built a whole movement dedicated to serving young girls and women. Think Like a Boss NJ is about learning how to be successful and teaching the next woman to do the same. With the motto of "No women left behind," we teach women different skills, host webinars, and even have summits on how to be a better you. It's one of the most fulfilling of all my ventures because it's not about me at all.

This is just a tip for your business but for your life overall. We were put here to be of service to others—we are a co-dependent species. So go out there and be the change you want to see.

"If you can speak, you can influence. If you can influence, you can change lives." — Rob Brown

TIP #17

BECOME A SPEAKER.

WANT TO BUILD A STRONG BRAND? BECOMING A SPEAKER is a golden opportunity to do this. You can take on the role of the teacher and the expert while showing your personality and sharing your story. It's the perfect mix of marketing, advertising, and branding.

In order to land some speaking engagements, start speaking at events in your community. These will not be paying engagements, but you'll be doing it for experience and exposure. From there, build a speaking packet. This packet should be equipped with pictures, a biography, press releases, speaker contract, and pricing information, to name a few things. See below for things you may want to include to make your packet stand out!

Biography: Make sure this is includes accolades, testimonies from past customers, press releases, books, and more.

FAQS Page: This should include speaking fees, where you will be traveling from, how you can assist in marketing the event, and what you may want or need to be included when you are asked to be a speaker.

Speaking Topics: This is a list of topics you can speak about as an expert, and you should explain whether you can alter the focus to cater to different organizations.

References: Include organizations or people that can vouch for your speaking abilities.

Speaking Inquiry Form: The organization should fill this out to give you elaborate details on their background, their event, and their expectations from you as a speaker.

Speaking Contract: The contract should include how payments should be made along with general terms and conditions that must be met for your bookings.

Travel Arrangements Form: This is form is important if you're traveling far for an event. This section should include airline and lodging information, mailing and shipping information for materials, and items that will be provided at the venue during your speaking time.

This just a generalized outline, so feel free to add any other information you may need. Once you have set up this professional packet, send your packet to events and organizations in your niche, get booked, and watch your brand recognition grow right before your eyes.

"Your calm mind is the ultimate weapon against
your challenges. So relax." — Bryant McGill

TIP #16

TAKE A BREAK.

CONGRATULATIONS, YOU'RE ALMOST HALFWAY THROUGH the 31 tips! This is the perfect time to advise you to take a break. Entrepreneurship is challenging and takes a lot of your time and energy, both mentally and physically. The last thing you want to happen is a burn-out. With that being said, take a vacation or take a few days off and gather yourself. Reconnect with family, with friends, and—most importantly—with yourself.

My break of choice is venturing off to a new place. Hence the creation of two more of my brands, I Am Travel Wear and www.TravelBittenLex.com. Traveling gives me the much needed rest from the CEO craziness, but traveling still fills me with inspiration and ideas while I play. The fulfillment, self-discovery, and enchantment of travel are reminders of why I want both the freedom and the success that entrepreneurship can bring.

So do yourself a favor and take a break. The well-deserved rest will get you back to where you need to be and will give you the fuel to go the extra miles that this journey will require.

"If your ship doesn't come in,
swim to it." — Unknown

TIP #15

CREATE YOUR
OWN OPPORTUNITIES.

AS AN EXTENSION OF TIP #18, IF EVENTS RELATED TO YOUR business are not common in your area, create your own! Become your own keynote speaker and start your own movement around your brand. This approach will gain you a huge following over time. You'll be able to control the creativity of the event, right down to the content being presented. As if that's not enough, you also get to sell your products and services to your audience.

Putting together events like these is no easy feat. This takes careful planning and an effective team for execution. As a CEO who plans annual Women Empowerment Summits for Think Like a Boss NJ, I am going to share all the tips and tricks. You did buy this book to learn, right?! I partnered with Curious (please see tip #21!) and put together a series of videos on "How to plan your own live event." Dive into this video at https://curious.com/actlikealadythinklikeaboss/series/how-to-plan-a-successful-live-event?ref=5ElX6-NdjGk #login

If you build it, they will come. So get out there and build your own opportunities.

"Life is a game. Money is how we score." – Unknown

TIP #14

GET SOME FUNDS!

SHOW ME THE MONEY!! I'M PRETTY SURE EVERY SMALL business, regardless of what stage they are in, is thinking this at one point or another. The reality is that funding is extremely hard to come by. Let's go over some ways you can go about getting some financial support to fund your dreams.

BORROWED MONEY

☐ **Personal savings**

☐ **Friends and relatives:** Use your support system!

- [ ] **Banks and credit unions:** Go through loan process with banks. (You will need your business plan!)

- [ ] **Microloan:** Micro lenders offer smaller loan sizes, usually require less documentation than banks and often apply more flexible underwriting criteria.

- [ ] **Venture capital firms:** These investors may fund your business expansion in exchange for partial ownership.

- [ ] **Crowdfunding:** This is a fun and effective way to raise money for a relatively low cost (e.g., GoFundMe).

- [ ] **Angel investor:** This is an individual who provides capital for a business start-up, in exchange for convertible debt or ownership equity (e.g., the TV show *Shark Tank*).

GRANTS AVAILABLE TO WOMEN, MINORITIES, AND SMALL BUSINESSES

- [ ] **The Eileen Fisher Women:** Woman-owned business grant program

- [ ] **Huggies Brand:** Mom-inspired grants

- [ ] **FedEx Think Bigger:** Small business grant

- [ ] **Idea Café:** Small business grant

- [ ] **Innovate Her:** Innovating Women business challenge

- [ ] **Chase Google:** Mission Main Street Project

- [ ] **Small Business Innovation Research (SBIR)**

- [ ] **Women Veteran Entrepreneur Corp (WVEC)**

- [ ] **Wal-Mart Women's Economic Empowerment Initiative (WEE):** - Small business competition

- [ ] **Zions Bank:** Smart Women, Smart Money

- [ ] **WomensNet.Net:** Amber grant for women

These are all great ways to raise funds for your business. It can be time consuming to research and pursue these options, but it is worth it in the end. When all else fails, default to Tip #27. I started my first company, The Evolution of Hip Hop LLC, with $1500 of my own money set aside from my 9-5 job. I used that money to put together a hip-hop event and doubled my investment on the proceeds. I then funneled that money back into the company for supplies, rent, and marketing. A month or two later my first customer walked through our door, looking for their unique dance party experience with The Evolution of Hip Hop. Whatever you do, don't give up.

"You are only as good as the people you hire." – Ray Kroc, Founder, McDonald's

TIP #13

HIRE AND FIRE PEOPLE.

EMPLOYEES CAN MAKE OR BREAK A COMPANY, BUT THE reality is that you need to hire employees in order to grow beyond your starting point. You have to eventually move away from tedious day-to-day activities that bog down your time. You need to be free to run, not walk, as you grow your company. This means you have to invest in talent.

This means you need to find the best person to do the job and to represent your brand in doing that job. You also have to invest in their development, and you have to show your appreciation by including them in your successes. A happy employee will do far more for the company than one that feels unappreciated in their job.

It is crucial to remember that these employees will affect both your productivity and your reputation. When you are experiencing growth, make sure you hire, and when someone is hindering your growth, don't be afraid to fire.

As a new or growing business, the money is not always going to be there to add new employees—and it may not be there for a while, so here's an extra tip for you. Hire a virtual assistant! A virtual assistant is a relatively low-cost, part-time contract employee who will help alleviate some of the tedious work that may be taking up some of your highly valuable time and preventing you from doing critical things for your company's growth. Look for services like Upwork (upwork.com), Freelancer (freelancer.com), or fiverr (fiverr.com) that have virtual assistants ready to work with different skill sets and hourly wages.

Make some changes, add people to your team, and flourish!

"It takes months to find a customer and only seconds to lose one." — Vince Lombardi

TIP #12

USE CUSTOMER SERVICE AS A SECRET WEAPON.

CUSTOMERS ARE YOUR BEST SOURCE OF ADVERTISEMENT.
Your customers make your business, and you have to treat them as such. Show them that you care, no matter your service or product. The quality of your service and how you make them feel will stick with them more than the price they paid. This is known as the "Starbucks effect." Starbucks created an environment that keeps their customers coming back. It starts with the way they ask for your name to personalize your order, and it extends to providing free Wi-Fi, power outlets for your electronic devices, and even dedicated phone-charging stations. You are so blown away by how they make you feel that you forget you paid $5 for a latte. Make sure

the quality of your service is impeccable, and the customer will feel like you are worth every penny.

The "Starbucks effect" works well for face-to-face interactions, but we have to remember customer service by phone and online. When your business operates primarily online, one of your best assets is speed. How quickly can you get back to a customer once they send an inquiry? In today's world, 24-48 hours is unacceptable, and I guarantee you your customers will be looking for an alternative if that's your response time. Your target timeframe should be immediately to about 4 hours; you have to cut that in half for social media. We are in the time of "I want it now," so the longer a customer waits, the higher the likelihood that you will lose that customer.

Another great piece of customer service advice is to be genuine and compassionate when dealing with the customers' issues or concerns. This further shows the personality of your brand. In addition to compassion, just give them the darn refund! Negative reviews online or on social media will hurt ten times worse than the cost of that refund you were fighting over.

Finally, stand out! If your business requires shipment of any products, you should be concerned about presentation and personalization of your shipping materials. Write a customer a note thanking them for their business in the best packaging that represents your brand, and that customer will be smiling from ear to ear when they open their package.

In a nutshell, go above and beyond for Mr. and Mrs. Customer, and word-of-mouth recommendations will enhance your brand and your business.

"You can make excuses and you can make money,
but you can't make both." – Ralph Oats

TIP #11

STOP MAKING EXCUSES.

THE BEST FRIEND OF FAILURE IS AN EXCUSE. THE TWO GO hand in hand and kill many dreams. Do yourself a favor and drop the excuses. If you dedicate the time you're wasting on excuses to building a plan, you'll be knee-deep into your dream. You DO have the time, you're NOT too tired, you DO know enough, and you CAN do it!!

"Don't be so thirsty for opportunity that you drink from every cup handed to you .... That's how you get poisoned." – Unknown

TIP #10

DON'T SELL YOURSELF SHORT.

EVERY OPPORTUNITY IS NOT FOR YOU, AND WHAT IS FOR you will not pass you by. Read each situation and opportunity clearly, and if you have any doubts in the morality of the project, people, or company, listen to your gut and let it pass you by. Never get to a point when you are so desperate for the next step that you put your business in a bad situation. Let your intuition guide you in what's best for you, your employees, and your business.

"Professionalism means consistency
of quality." – Frank Tyger

TIP #9

PAY THE EXTRA MONEY FOR PROFESSIONALISM.

HOW MANY TIMES HAVE YOU VISITED A WEBSITE TO DO research and turned back once you saw how unprofessional it seemed? In this day and age, with the sleekness of Apple and the functionality of Android, we realize that the masses are attracted to well-crafted and professionally designed pieces of work. You must apply the same thinking to your company. Unless you are a web programmer, a graphic designer, a business-oriented marketer, and a pro photographer, invest in professional services to build an excellent website, design a brilliant logo, create memorable business cards, and collect a portfolio of high-quality photography, all the way down to a purchasing attractive uniforms. Even if you have the skills for one or two of these items, you have other important things to do to get your business going. So, whatever your company needs, make sure it's both functional and appealing.

One feature that new companies lack is a professional phone number. With companies like RingCentral that charge less than $25 a month for their robust services, there is no reason why your cell phone number has to be your business number. You can set up a number and even tie it to all your employees' phones or your cell. It has separate services like voice recording, different extensions, office hours, automated messages, and more.

This is no longer your hobby, this is your business. It's time to look, sound, and feel like a business.

"Keep your mind young by continuing to learn about your business." – Frank Bettger

TIP #8

KNOW YOUR COMPANY'S DNA.

AFTER THE FIRST TWO YEARS IN OPERATION YOU SHOULD have an idea of best practices when it comes to your business. Most importantly you should know the trends, high and low monthly revenues, and which holidays work with you or against you.

Knowing your business inside and out will not only help you plan accordingly for the year, but if you share this knowledge it's also helpful for employees and customers alike. For onboarding new employees, you should have documentation of procedures for handling problems that arise, of scripts for sales and customer service, or directions for products.

Training your employees will be much easier with less repetition and more reference material.

It's a similar situation for the customer. In two years, just about everything that could happen will have happened, and all kinds of questions will have been asked by customers. You should keep track of these questions and issues, so you can improve both your products and your service in support of your products. When you see a trend in questions and problems, create a Frequently Asked Questions (FAQs) page that covers the most common inquiries that are asked when it comes to your products or services. This will save you time on customer calls and emails that may be focused on the same question you've been getting from day one.

"Stay hungry, stay foolish." — *Steve Jobs*

TIP #7

NEVER STAY SATISFIED WITH YOUR LAST ACCOMPLISHMENT.

WHEN YOU BECOME A BUSINESS OWNER, YOUR BUSINESS immediately has one competitor. That competitor is you. Year over year you should be finding new ways to outdo yourself and reach new heights. A big win in January won't mean anything in 365 days. Never stay content or get comfortable with current victories. Complacency can lead to mistakes, missed opportunities, and failures. Celebrate, move on, and keep hunting.

*"The person you blow off in life may have
the secret to your success." – Unknown*

TIP #6

BECOME A
PEOPLE PERSON.

WE BRIEFLY SPOKE ABOUT DIFFERENT AVENUES FOR
working with others. The importance of partnership, networking, community programs, and employees relies on how you treat others. The whole world of business comes down to human relationships. Like the saying says, you catch more flies with honey. Do your best to be impactful with people you meet. Remember their names, ask them about their dreams … but most importantly listen to them with the intent to actually hear them and not just to respond. That way you can close the circle of communication and build stronger and more memorable connections.

Some of my biggest opportunities have come from meaningful conversations I've had, some of them just an hour or even 30 minutes. By sharing my story and genuinely listening while someone else shared theirs, I was able to book some substantial work. For example, at one point I was on a set working with Alec Baldwin, and I connected with a crew member as we talked in general about dreams and ideas. Three months later I received an email saying, "After meeting you and your personality on set, I think you would be a perfect fit for this—good luck." Attached to the email was an application looking for unique and boisterous personalities for a remake of the iconic show *The $100,000 Pyramid*, with Michael Strahan as the new host. From there, history was made. I was one of the first contestants on the first season. With a focused mind and a grateful heart, I made $60,000 in 30 minutes in front of approximately 6 million people! It didn't end there, either! On the set of *The $100,000 Pyramid*, I hit it off with another crew member, and we spoke about life, dreams, and even zodiac signs! Four months later this crew member found me through my company's website. She remembered our conversation and thought I would be a great fit for an international commercial showcasing people who weren't afraid to follow their dreams. This was a commercial that was perfect for me since I've been doing this my whole life. I booked the audition and was back in front of the camera.

We are all connected to one another. Once you're in someone's presence, make it count because people always remember the way you make them feel. Don't blow people off with a negative attitude or speak only to people you deem worthy of your time. It doesn't matter if they're the janitor, mailroom clerk, stage manager, host, sales rep, or CEO … be kind always. They can change your life or—even better—you can change theirs.

"Longevity means we have to evolve, that we have to change and be able to change." – Wolfgang Puck

TIP #5

REINVENT YOURSELF.

TIMES CHANGE, TRENDS CHANGE, AND YOU HAVE TO change, too. With the ever-growing world of technology, the ways in which people receive their information, service, and products are always changing. If you don't change with the times, you will be left behind. Look at movie rental giant Blockbuster as an example. They had the movie rental industry locked down. Every Thursday through Sunday, every local Blockbuster was packed, and holidays were ten times worse. Then a small company named Netflix came along and capitalized on sending your video rentals straight to your home. The video juggernaut had the capability to do the same but decided to focus just on what they were good at: having you come in rent videos and accrue late fees if you didn't return the videos on time. Netflix, however, didn't stick with just mailing movies to you—they added a new service to allow you to stream movies online. By the time Blockbuster tried to catch up, it was too late: Netflix had taken over a large percentage of the customer mindshare in that space. Now Blockbuster is completely out of business and several years' later people are using the term "Netflix and chill".

Don't get blockbusted out of your industry! Add new products and services as customers' needs start to change. Don't get so arrogant in your space that you start to oppose new ideas. Try to diversify to new areas in your business to attract new customers while keeping old customers engaged.

"Getting a mentor is the shortcut to success." — Bo Sanchez

TIP #4

GET A MENTOR.

EVEN THOUGH THIS IS YOUR JOURNEY, YOU DON'T HAVE to travel alone. Build a relationship with someone who has been there and done that. If they are truly successful, they will not have a problem sharing tips and tricks of the trade. Most successful people have had a mentor or two who have contributed to their success. Take the legendary Oprah Winfrey: In her hardest times, she picked up the phone and called her mentor, the late great Maya Angelou, for advice and direction. Get yourself a mentor—pick their brains, pick up great habits and techniques from their successes, and learn through their mistakes, your walk to the top can be an easier one with someone guiding you.

"The difference between ordinary and extraordinary is that little extra." – Jimmy Johnson

TIP #3

TAKE THE LEAP AND BE EXTRAORDINARY.

WHEN YOU SETTLE FOR THE ORDINARY DAY WITH ORDInary choices that all ordinary people make, you will live an ordinary life. When you break the mold and make an extraordinary choice that ordinary people would never make, that is when you will live an extraordinary life. Deciding to follow your dreams is an extraordinary choice, and extraordinary actions will be needed to make that choice a reality. The universe will always give back what you put out, so stop putting out mediocrity. No amount of security or comfort of routine is worth the destruction of your dreams. Break the shackles of the ordinary and be extraordinary!

"If they don't know you personally, don't take it personally." — Unknown

TIP #2

DON'T TAKE IT PERSONALLY.

THIS LESSON IS TAUGHT IN SALES 101. YOU NEED TO HAVE tough skin when it comes to growing your business. You're going to hear words like "No," "Not at this time," and "I'm not interested" at every stage of your business. This may deter you, but do not allow this to slow you down. The law of probability states you will get many NO's before a YES even presents itself. Along the road of success you will run into people who do not believe in your product, banks that won't lend you any money, and family and friends who won't support you. This has NOTHING to do with you or your dream. Keep pushing through; this is where grit and perseverance is needed. Take each blow with a grain of salt and add it to your brew of success!

"When the storm comes, your why keeps you anchored. Know your why and you'll always have something to keep you grounded." – Alexandra

TIP #1

REMEMBER YOUR WHY.

YOU WILL FAIL, YOU WILL STUMBLE, YOU WILL GET FRUStrated, you will get discouraged, you will get tired, you will want to give up—so what will keep you grounded? Why are you doing this? What is the big picture? Freedom? Happiness? Security? Your legacy? To change the world? Whatever it is, make sure it's strong enough to keep you motivated. You'll need it to draw inspiration from every now and then. If the **why** is simply money, that's not enough. Anyone can make money, but not everyone can make money AND be happy from the inside out. Find your anchor and stay grounded.

CONCLUSION

IN THIS ADVENTURE CALLED LIFE, THERE IS ONLY ONE PER-
son who knows what is best for you and your life. That person is you. We
all have an internal compass. When your heart and soul are set on a desti-
nation, your mind and strong intention will design a map to get you there.
Use these tips, heed the advice, work diligently, and stay focused. Fear
comes from the lack of knowledge. That is not you. Go out there and allow
your greatness to change the world.